ETHICS 1

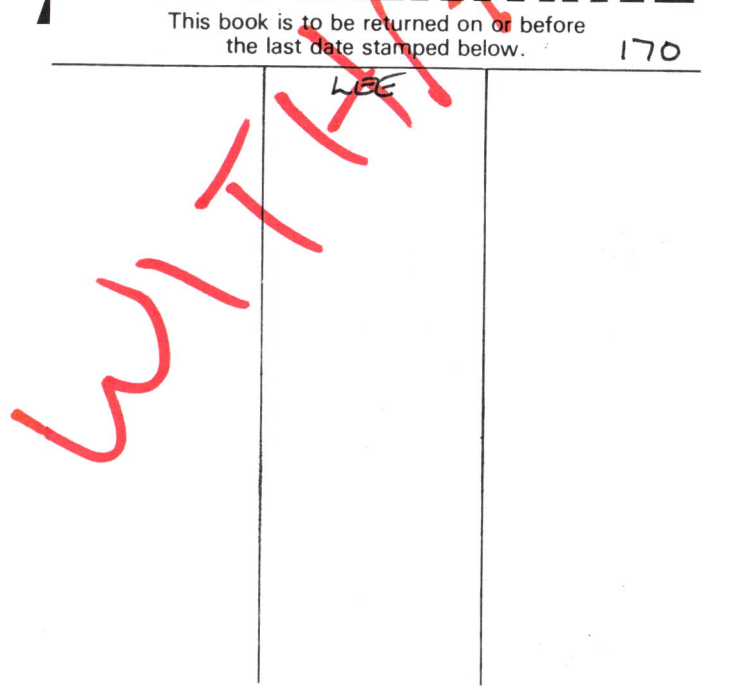

ETHICAL THEORY AND LANGUAGE

170

This booklet is copyright and may not be copied or reproduced, in whole or in part, by any means, without the publisher's prior written consent.

© Copyright 1999
First published 1999

Abacus Educational Services
424 Birmingham Road
Marlbrook
Bromsgrove
Worcestershire
B61 0HL

ISBN 1 898653 14 3

Other titles available in the series:
    2.   Moral Rules
    3.   Christian Ethics (in preparation)
    4.   Homosexuality

Also available:

Philosophy of Religion series:
    1.   Religious Language
    2.   The Problem of Evil
    3.   Faith and Reason
    4.   God and Proof
    5.   Revelation and Religious Experience
    6.   Life after Death
    7.   Miracles

Other titles on the Synoptic Gospels and the Fourth Gospel are also available.

CONTENTS

INTRODUCTION	4
WHAT IS ETHICS?	5
WHAT DO ALL THE ETHICAL TERMS MEAN?	7
WHAT DOES THE WORD 'RIGHT' MEAN?	11
WHAT IS THE DIFFERENCE BETWEEN 'RIGHT' AND 'GOOD'?	26
WHAT IS THE NATURE OF MORAL LANGUAGE?	27
SHOULD WE ACT MORALLY?	29
WORKSHEET	32
EXAM QUESTIONS	34
FURTHER READING	36
GLOSSARY	38

INTRODUCTION

This booklet has been written specifically to cater for the needs of A/AS students of Philosophy and Religious Studies. However, it may equally be used as an introduction to ethics by the interested lay person or by first year undergraduates.

The style of the booklet is similar to the style employed in other booklets in other series. It is structured around key questions that have developed from classroom experience. It also contains a section that deals with exam questions and should therefore be useful for both teaching and revision.

Philosophy, of which ethics is a part, can be great fun to both study and to teach. It is a subject that both staff and students can become fully engaged in. It is therefore hoped that learning about ethics will prove to be an enjoyable experience.

WHAT IS ETHICS?

It is probable that everyone at some point has become involved in an 'ethical' debate. If you have ever discussed what you think should be done about environmental problems or whether people should be vegetarian, you have been involved with ethics. If you have ever expressed an opinion about abortion, euthanasia or drug taking, you have been involved with ethics. Even if you have reacted to someone on the news because you think that she/he has done something wrong, then you have been involved in ethics.

Ethics, put simply, is about deciding what is right or wrong. So stating, for example, that you think that murder is wrong, is to give an ethical opinion. However, in Philosophy ethics isn't solely concerned with practical issues, like, for example, whether war can ever be acceptable, it is also concerned with the *theory*: are there any rules for deciding what is right and wrong? What does the word 'good' mean? Is it different from the word 'right'? Is there any reason for acting morally in the first place?

Traditionally philosophers have divided ethics into three main areas. All three areas approach the subject differently but all interrelate with each other.

▶ 1. Metaethics

This is the study of the nature of morality. In many ways this is where the meaning of ethical terms is discussed. For example, in metaethics the question 'what does 'right' mean?' could be examined.

Metaethics also deals with questions like whether morals (statements about ethics) are true or false like statements about facts, or whether morals are simply statements of opinions. In other words, does 'right' always mean the same thing?

One way of seeing metaethics is to imagine you are stepping back from an ethical debate for a moment: what do the terms you are using mean? Would they mean the same if you were involved in another debate? These are obviously crucial questions because any philosopher's answers to metaethical questions will affect what she/he thinks about other issues.

▶ 2. Normative ethics.

The word 'normative' comes from the word 'norm' which means rule (in the sense of rules for a game). Basically normative ethics is the area in which philosophers discuss whether there are any rules for determining whether something is right or wrong. It asks the question: what is it right for people to do? (What ought we do?)

Note that these sorts of questions are general. They are about principles not specific instances. Again conclusions drawn in normative ethics will influence what philosophers have to say about any moral issue.

▶ 3. Practical ethics.

Practical ethics is often called Applied ethics. It is the area of ethics that applies theory to practical (real) situations. It is the area in which most people at some time may have expressed an opinion. For example, practical ethics includes issues such as euthanasia and animal rights and considers questions like: is lying ever acceptable? Is suicide morally wrong?

It is important to remember that whilst anyone can give an opinion on any of these issues, in philosophy it is essential to recognize the theoretical background. For example, stating that some people believe that abortion is wrong because it is equivalent to murder is a powerful argument but it is only the beginning: a discussion of whether something is always wrong in any situation, for example, would enhance any response.

Indeed the question as to whether abortion is wrong is a good example of what the different parts of ethics are about: metaethics would give an understanding of what 'wrong' means; normative ethics would give an understanding of whether there are any general rules that need to be followed in order to determine whether abortion is wrong; and finally in practical ethics these ideas will be applied in order to fully answer the question.

WHAT DO ALL THE ETHICAL TERMS MEAN?

One of the most difficult things about reading any books on ethics, particularly ethical theory, is the quantity and variety of ethical terms: there seems to be a word or 'ism' for any possible position or opinion; and further some writers seem to favour different terms.

The following is an outline of some of the key terms found in ethics. They will mostly be referred to later and the following is really a checklist which can be looked back at.

▶ **Ethics and morality.**

One of the most immediate clarifications needed is in the subject title itself. The words 'ethics' and 'morals' have already been used, is there any difference between them? Ethics is often defined as 'the science of morals'. In other words ethics is the study of morals and morality. Both these words are about what is right and wrong and how everyone should behave. They are thus interchangeable. Some writers do prefer the word 'ethics' to describe the academic study of morals whereas others tend to call this area of philosophy 'moral philosophy'.

▶ **Cognitive and Non-Cognitive.**

These two terms are basically at the heart of metaethics. 'Cognition' is a word that refers to thought and awareness. So if something is 'cognitive' it can be known or perceived. In contrast, to describe something as 'non-cognitive' would mean that it was neither true nor false; it could, for example, refer to an emotion or opinion.

Basically in metaethics there are two possible types of response as to what 'right' might mean. One considers that morals can be true or false: they can (somehow) be perceived to be true or false. In other words morals are facts. This view is known as cognitivism because it suggests that morals can be perceived. In contrast some philosophers have suggested that morals are not facts. Instead morals are about opinions or expressions of feelings. This view is known as non-cognitivism because it suggests that right and wrong are not things that can be perceived.

Consider, for example, Caroline who has witnessed something in the street, she describes: it was in Clacton-on-sea; it was four o'clock in the afternoon; the woman stabbed the man in the stomach; the man died. These are all facts about what Caroline has seen. The cognitivist would argue that if Caroline were to add the description that this action was wrong, then this is another fact about the action: it is a fact in the same way the saying that it was four o'clock is a fact. (Though it should be noted that Caroline could be wrong about either of these facts.) In contrast, the non-cognitivist would argue that if Caroline were to say that the action was wrong, then really all that she is saying is that she disapproves of the action: it is an opinion not a fact.

▶**Objective and subjective.**

In many ways these two terms are very similar in meaning to the ideas of cognitivism and non-cognitivism. 'Objective' means to exist independently of thought; or in other words to describe something as objective is to say that it is really there. In contrast 'subjective' means dependent on thought; this thought is most usually an emotion. One way of seeing this distinction is to see 'objective' as external and 'subjective' as internal. For example, consider the difference between: 'this beach is covered in sand' and 'this beach is my favourite place'. The first statement is objective, the beach would have sand whether I existed or not, whereas the second statement is subjective, it depends on what I think about the beach.

Thus, in ethics, morals have been either described as objective or subjective. If they are objective, then they are true for everyone. This theory is called objectivism. If they are subjective, then they are dependent on our own views, opinions or feelings. This view is called subjectivism.

▶**Descriptive and prescriptive.**

These two terms are essentially a way of explaining what ethics does and consequently what ethical terms mean. If you describe something, you say what it is like. Whereas if you prescribe something, you say how it should be or what ought to be done. Thus in ethics there are two ways of seeing what ethics does. The first is that ethical terms are descriptive i.e. they describe something. The other is that ethical terms are prescriptive i.e. they give commands about what people ought to do.

Take the example of murder. If ethics is descriptive, then murder may be wrong because there is something in or about the act of murder that is wrong: part of the description of murder is to say that it is wrong. In contrast if ethics is prescriptive, then someone might say that murder is wrong because that is not the behaviour that she/he thinks is acceptable: it is not the sort of behaviour that she/he would prescribe.

This is a distinction that is slightly different to the one between cognitive and non-cognitive. Indeed cognitive ethical theories, for example, may either be descriptive or prescriptive.

Absolute and relative.

If something is absolute, then it is true in all situations. If something is relative, then it is dependent on circumstances. These two terms are another way of dividing up ethical theory. Some theories suggest that morals are absolute or in other words if something is right for one person in one situation, then it must be true for all people in all situations. So, for example, if someone were to say that lying is wrong, it would have to be wrong regardless of the circumstances. This belief is called absolutism: morals are absolutes. In contrast other theories suggest that the circumstances and situation do make a difference and consequently something, such as lying, might be wrong in one situation but acceptable in another. Such theories are known as relativism: the moral truth of something is relative to the situation.

Ends and means (Deontological and Teleological).

An end is an outcome or something that you achieve. Whereas the means is the way that something is achieved. These two terms are really important in normative ethics. Some moral philosophers argue that what is important in ethics is the ends i.e. it is what you achieve that is important not how you achieve it. In contrast to this other moral philosophers argue that the end result is not the important aspect of ethics it is what you do (the means) and what rules that you follow which determine whether something is right or wrong.

As an example consider the situation where you want to help your poor and elderly neighbour. You could do this by going to the supermarket and stealing her some food. Some moral philosophers would argue that this could be the right thing to do as the end product (the full stomach of your neighbour) is a good thing. Others, however, would disagree and would argue that your action was wrong as the means you used (theft) are not, and can never be, acceptable.

There are also some longer terms used in ethics to describe theories based on ends and means. They are 'deontological' and 'teleological'. 'Deontological' literally means 'concerned with duty' and theories are described as deontological if they are concerned with means or in other words if they argue that something is wrong because of how you do it. 'Teleological' literally means 'concerned with ends' and theories are described as teleological if they describe something as wrong if the consequence of the action is bad. Indeed such a theory is sometimes also known as *Consequentialism*. (Something is wrong or right because of the consequences.)

WHAT DOES THE WORD 'RIGHT' MEAN?

Most people have a reasonable idea as to what the word 'right' means: most people can happily use the word in everyday language. Indeed it is used in a variety of ways and in a variety of contexts. Ignoring the 'other' definitions of right—such as opposite to left—in ethics 'right' could be defined as what is morally acceptable. This, however, does not really add to the understanding of right as there is much discussion as to what is and is not morally acceptable. Put simply philosophers agree on the general meaning of the word but disagree as to what this general meaning implies.

As has already been discussed, there are really two different sorts of way in which the word 'right' could be defined. One of these is to state that 'right' is some sort of fact, like 'I am 6 feet tall' is a fact. The other is to state that 'right' is some sort of opinion, like 'Whisky is the best drink in the world' is an opinion.

The whole area of defining right is a very complex area and really there are many different approaches that could be taken. The distinction between cognitive and non-cognitive is in some ways rather artificial as the distinction is relatively modern and many ethical theories were not developed with it in mind.

▶RIGHT AS FACT. (Cognitivism)

There are many different theories that fit into this category. The main ones are: Naturalism, Intuitionism and Prescriptivism. The first one of these also divides into a number of sub-theories.

▶1. Naturalism.

Any theory or philosopher that argues that morals can be reduced to some aspect of nature could be described as naturalistic. Naturalism, in ethics, is the belief that ethics and ethical language can be deduced from looking at nature. In other words morals are observable in or deducible from nature. Nature here means either the natural world and/or human beings. Thus right (and wrong) is a feature of the natural world or of the nature of human beings; and what is right can be determined by looking at these things. Such theories see ethics as descriptive.

Naturalism is really a general title given to different theories.

▶ (a) Hedonism. ('Right is what gives pleasure.')

The first thing to note is that Hedonism is a development of a different ethical theory known as Egoism. Egoism is the belief that human beings are only interested in themselves and their own ends. In other words it is the belief that whatever anyone does it is for her/his own benefit. Thus in terms of right an Egoist might define right as 'whatever is in our own interest.' However, there is an immediate problem with this view as it may not be immediately obvious as to what is in our interest. Hedonism attempts to answer this problem by asserting that self-interest is based on pleasure. The theory of Egoism will be discussed further in the section entitled *Should we act morally?*

Hedonism itself is an ancient ethical theory. In everyday language 'hedonism' means the pursuit of pleasure. In ethical theory Hedonism is a position which states that the only thing that is right is pleasure. Everyone, the hedonist argues, is interested in getting for herself/himself the maximum amount of pleasure. For the hedonist it is self-evident that everyone will want to do this because it is illogical for anyone not to want to experience pleasure.

Thus right is defined, for the hedonist, in terms of an aspect of human nature: that part of human nature that enjoys pleasure. An action or thing is considered right if it brings about pleasure (or indeed avoids pain) and is considered wrong if it fails to bring about pleasure or causes pain.

Criticisms

— The most obvious point that is often made against hedonism is that it rules out a lot of things that most people consider to be right. What about Rachel who wants to help an old person with her shopping? A lot of people would consider this action to be right even though it seems to be ruled out by hedonism. However, hedonism can be more sophisticated than this as the action can be right because it may give Rachel pleasure to help others. Indeed she may get a lot of benefits (i.e. pleasure) from it, such as friendship with the person she helps.

—There are, however, more significant criticisms of hedonism. Firstly, there is a problem trying to say what pleasure is. It seems that it could be different for everyone. For example, Rachel likes chocolate, you may not. This can lead to logical inconsistencies. Consider people who enjoy giving pain to other people (they are called sadists). Are their actions right or wrong? The hedonist has to say both because the action is bringing about pleasure and bringing about pain.

—Further, it could be argued that sometimes pain can be right . It is for Rachel's own good, for example, that she visits the dentist after eating all the chocolate: this is a painful experience, and therefore wrong according to hedonists, but it does bring about some longer term benefits.

▶**(b) Utilitarianism. ('Right is the greatest happiness of the greatest number.')**

Utilitarianism is a very important and historically significant ethical theory that will be discussed at length in the second booklet in this series. For the purposes of this section it is important to recognize that Utilitarians have also given a definition of right. In many ways Utilitarianism is a development of hedonism. However, a slightly wider rule has been developed to determine whether something is right: does it bring about the greatest happiness of the greatest number? Or, in other words, has the maximum amount of happiness been created by the action?

The specific problems associated with Utilitarianism will also be discussed in the second booklet in this series. However, some of the criticisms of hedonism, such as pain can be pleasure also apply to Utilitarianism.

▶**(c) Scientific reductionism. ('Right is a fact of biology, sociology or psychology.')**

One 20th century development in ethics has been the attempt by some philosophers to reduce or explain morals in terms of something else. There are three main areas that philosophers have attempted to reduce ethics to: Biology, Psychology and Sociology.

With regards to biology some philosophers have attempted to explain moral language in terms of Evolution. Hence the fact that this theory is sometimes called Evolutionary ethics. It is argued that humans are animals and, consequently, that morals are another way of describing the behaviour of the human species. Part of the purpose of human behaviour, and hence moral behaviour, is to ensure the survival of the species. Thus to say an action is right is to say that the behaviour does promote the survival of the species i.e. it promotes evolution.

Approaches from Psychology and Sociology are very similar. In terms of Psychology, morality might be seen as a way of expressing an individual's sexuality or fear, for example. In other words morals may be ways of expressing unconscious motives. Alternatively, morals may be a way of describing class struggle or the way in which one class may think that another is wrong. This is an idea developed from Sociology. Both these 'reductions' are actually based on theories found in Psychology and Sociology (in this case Freud and Marx): other theories may lead to different explanations of what morality is. However, in both what is important is that morals become facts of behaviour, mind, or society and thus can be described.

Criticisms

—There are some specific criticisms of each of the three different areas, but one general criticism of all three tends to be that they are two narrow: attempting to reduce morality to one area of human life, it is argued, misses out on the importance of other areas.

—It is also argued that if ethics is reduced to science, then presumably what is right and wrong can be known in the same way that facts about science can be known. This does not, however, seem to be the case. Ethical problems do not seem to be 'solved' in the same way that problems in science are; people still disagree as to what is right and wrong. Indeed this problem is at the heart of the main criticisms of any Naturalistic theory.

▶ d) The Interest of the Stronger. ('Might is right.')

Another ancient theory that could be seen to be a form of naturalism, and which attempts to define right, is based on the idea of power. This theory appears in the Greek philosopher Plato's book The Republic which was written at least 350 years before the birth of Jesus. The Republic is essentially a discussion as to what justice is and this is a theory that Plato discusses and then rejects. It is argued that what is right is whatever is in the interest of the stronger party. In other words what is right is defined in terms of who has power: right has no other meaning than this. Thus whatever the most powerful say is right is right, hence the slogan 'might is right'. This could be the reason, for example, that things such as taxes are right: they are in the interest of those in power.

This theory could in some ways be linked to the Sociological theories just considered. It is cognitive because 'right' is still a fact, what is in the interest of the stronger party. However, whilst there are echoes of this theory in many more modern writings, these theories tend to be non-cognitive. (See later.)

Criticisms.

—The biggest criticism of this theory has been that it makes no distinction between right and power. It seems obvious to most people that you can be powerful without necessarily being right. Similarly the powerful, for example, might make rules or laws that people don't think are right. If I was in power, for example, I could make the rule that everyone has to hand over all her/his chocolate to me. Many people would say that this action was wrong, but it doesn't make sense for them to say that, if the theory is correct, since power equals right.

▶ Criticisms of Naturalism

—*Facts and values are different.* One major criticism of Naturalism has been that facts and values are different. Many philosophers have argued that moral language is of a different order to factual language: moral language does not describe in the same way that factual language does. For example, the critic of Naturalism might argue that the sentences 'Murder is most widespread in Colombia' and 'Murder is wrong' are different in quality: one is a fact the other is not.

—*Hume's law.* Another way of expressing this criticism is to say that describing the facts of any situation never leads to making a value judgement. For example, someone could describe every single detail of a murder but if she/he said that murder was wrong, then this would be to add something more than a description. This is often known as Hume's Law (after the 18th Century, Scottish philosopher David Hume) which states that 'what is' does not imply what ought to be.

—*Moore: Naturalistic fallacy.* A major critic of Naturalism was the British philosopher G.E. Moore (1873–1958). He argued that it is wrong to identify morality with any other concept. In other words to say that morality is something else is not acceptable. Consider, for example, Hedonism that states that right is happiness. Moore argued that it was wrong to do this and attempt to do so was a mistake in reasoning: a poor argument. The reason for this, according to Moore, is that any attempt to translate moral terms into something else will miss out some important aspect or meaning of those terms. A mistake in reasoning is often called a fallacy and thus Moore's criticism is called the Naturalistic fallacy.

—*Open question argument.* The 'open question argument' is another way of seeing the supposed fallacy in attempting to identify moral terms with something natural. Indeed it can be seen as the reason why it would be a fallacy to do this. Suppose, for example, someone accepted the Hedonist belief that what is right is what gives pleasure. A particular action, maybe eating chocolate, gives her/him pleasure but it can still be asked whether that action is right. It still makes sense to ask that question. It is an 'open' question because it can still be given an answer even though the answer should be obvious if Naturalism is true. In other words the question as to whether an action is right can still be asked even if that action fits in with a Naturalistic theory. [Consider Reuben the Hedonist. He enjoys eating meat. He could be asked: does eating meat give you pleasure? Reuben would say that it did. Now if right means pleasure (which is the heart of Hedonism), then Reuben has already said that his action is right. However, it does seem to make sense to go on to ask Reuben whether he thinks eating meat is the right thing.]

—*What is natural?* A different type of criticism of Naturalism has been to question whether there is anything natural in the first place. The human understanding of nature and what is considered 'natural' changes. Does this mean that ethics changes? Indeed some philosophers have gone further and argued that there is no such thing as human nature and therefore nothing to base any theory of Naturalism on.

2. Intuitionism ('Right is obvious: it is known through intuition.')

Intuitionism is an ethical theory that was developed by Moore in response to the problems he thought there were with Naturalism. Moore still believed that moral language was cognitive i.e. that it was factual and meaningful. However, it was not based on something from nature but on intuition. An intuition is a direct kind of knowledge. You know something through intuition directly: it is not something you have worked out or experienced. (One of the most common ways the word is used in everyday language is the remarkable way many people seem to know what someone else is thinking. They haven't worked it out nor have they been told. It is known through intuition.)

Moore argued that morals are obvious: everyone knows by intuition what is right or wrong. If you were to consider a moral problem, and once you have weighed up the evidence, the right course of action should be obvious. This is a similar idea to other philosophers who have attempted to argue that ethics is based on conscience i.e. there is some inner sense in humans by which they know what is right or wrong.

Criticisms of Intuitionism.

—*What if two people come to different conclusions?* One of the biggest problems with Intuitionism is that there is no way of determining who is right if two people conclude, through intuition, opposing views. You could, for example, think you know through intuition that war is wrong: it may be obvious to you. However, it may also appear obvious to someone else that war is acceptable.

Intuitionism does not seem to provide an immediate solution to this problem.

—*What or who guarantees that intuitions are 'correct'?* In many ways this is related to the first problem. Intuition seems to demand that there is some agency that ensures that what is concluded through intuition is correct, otherwise intuition becomes not much more than gut feeling. However, what could this be? It could be God. This would, however, introduce a rather large philosophical assumption into the theory.

—*Intuition is meaningless.* Other philosophers have argued that the whole idea of intuition does not make sense. They have questioned what it is and whether any account of how it works can be given.

▶ 3. Prescriptivism. ('Right is an instruction.')

This is a theory most notably developed by the 20th Century philosopher R.M. Hare and in many ways can be seen likened to the ideas of Kant (whose ethical theories will be considered in the second booklet in this series). Hare argued that moral language is descriptive but it is also more than that. Moral language is not simply about any 'natural' property it is also prescriptive. In other words it also gives instructions and guidance to others. A prescriptive statement is one that gives instruction as to how things should be. For example, 'shut that door' is a prescriptive statement because it gives a command to change the situation from door open to door closed. Thus what Hare argued was that a prescriptive meaning of moral terms needed to be added to the descriptive meaning. In terms of right, Hare argued that if someone said what she/he thought was right, she/he would not just be saying how the word should be used but she/he is also giving moral instruction.

However, Hare argued that whilst moral judgements are prescriptive they are different from other commands (such as 'shut the door') because they are *universalizable*. This means that the person giving the instruction wishes the instruction to be true for all people in all situations. For example, there is a difference between saying 'pass the salt' and 'don't lie' because the first is only a command in a particular situation whereas the speaker in the second, according to Hare, wishes that to be the case in all situations. This idea of universalizability is what makes moral language different from other types of language.

▶ Criticisms of Prescriptivism.

—*What is added?* The main criticism of Prescriptivism, other than the general criticisms of cognitive theories, has been that there does not seem to be much added to the meaning of the word 'right' by giving it a prescriptive meaning. How is my understanding of the word right enhanced by seeing it as an instruction to act as well as a description of what is? [Think about this. Isn't there a tension between description and prescription? Doesn't something prescriptive have to necessarily become non-cognitive i.e. an opinion? If it isn't an opinion, what is it?]

▶ 4. God. ('Right is what God wills.)

This is a very different approach to the other ethical theories that have already been examined. Essentially this view is at the heart of Christian ethics (which will be discussed at length in the third booklet in this series). Many Christians, and other religious groups, argue that whatever God says is right is right. Thus the meaning of right is whatever God decides that it is.

▶ Criticisms of God as the basis of ethics.

—*Does God exist?* The most immediate problem with this theory is that it rests on the assumption that God exists. If you do not believe this, then the theory obviously cannot be true.

—*How can God's commands be known?* A second problem, and one that has been a major discussion within Christianity, has been how can human beings know what God has decided is right? A number of responses have been suggested to this problem, such as that God has revealed Himself through the Bible and that human beings can work it out through the use of reason. However, it is not clear how anyone should respond if there is a difference between these two solutions.

—*Might there be a contradiction?* A more sophisticated problem with the idea that God is the author of what is right is to question whether such a view leads to a contradiction. If God can decide whatever He wants to be right, He could choose something that is harmful to human beings. However, this goes against what many people believe to be right. In contrast, if God cannot choose anything to be right, then the word right must be defined in terms of something other than God.

▶ Right as Feeling. (Non-cognitivism)

As has already been said the contrast to arguing that right is some sort of fact is to suggest that right is a feeling or emotion. Such an approach reduces ethics to a personal opinion. Theories that do this are labelled subjectivist because they are based on the individual (the subject). *Subjectivism* is any theory that says that the truth of something is dependent on an individual point of view. Thus ethical subjectivism is the view that the truth of moral statements are dependent on opinions. In other words right is *'what I think of something'*.

However, this position of ethical subjectivism does not really give an explanation as to what is being done when someone makes an ethical judgement i.e. what constitutes an 'opinion' needs explaining. Two developments of subjectivism do do this: Emotivism and Relativism.

▶ 1. Emotivism. ('Right is an expression of emotion.')

Emotivism is a theory that was most notably developed by the 20th Century English philosopher A. J. Ayer (1910-1989) and an expression of it can be found in his book *Language, Truth and Logic*. In order to fully understand what Ayer was arguing it is important to understand a little bit more about his general philosophy. Part of Ayer's aim was to analyse what gives something meaning or, in other words, what the meaning of meaning is. Ayer believed that a statement could only be meaningful if it could be verified i.e. you could use your senses in some way to determine whether the statement is true. (Consider the statements: 'There is a computer in this room' and 'There is an invisible monster in this room'. The first can be verified (checked out) and is, therefore, according to Ayer, meaningful; the second cannot be verified and is therefore meaningless.) Meaningful statements are described by Ayer as 'scientific'. However, he does recognize that there are non-literal statements, such as expressions of emotion: these do not need to be verifiable because they are neither true nor false. In other words Ayer thought that there were two types of statement: facts and opinions. The first had to be verifiable; the second were not factually significant. (For a fuller discussion of Ayer's view of language, see the booklet entitled *Religious Language* in the philosophy of religion series.)

Ayer went on to apply his theory of meaning to moral language and concluded that morals could not be facts. He rejected the theories of naturalism for very similar reasons to Moore (see above). However, he also rejected Intuitionism. His reason for this was that he believed that intuitions were unverifiable (and therefore, according to his philosophy of meaning, were meaningless.) Ayer argued that moral statements did not add anything to a situation, all they did was to express disapproval of an action. For example, Ayer would have argued that to say 'you acted wrongly' adds no fact to the statement 'you killed the baby': all it is is another way of saying 'I disapprove of your action'. For Ayer 'right' and 'wrong' are not words that can be factually correct or incorrect. Instead they are absolutely identical in meaning to 'I approve of what you are doing' or 'I disapprove of what you are doing'.

Thus for Ayer moral statements are expressions of emotion (approval or disapproval); and hence the theory is known as Emotivism. It has also been described as the 'Hurrah-boo' theory of morals. If I approve of something, it is right (Hurrah!). If I disapprove of something, then it is wrong (Boo!).

However, Ayer argued that moral statements were not just about meaning they were also about wanting others to behave how we want to. Thus 'killing the baby is wrong' is a statement that means 'I disapprove of killing the baby' but it is also my instruction: 'I do not want you to kill the baby'. Moral statements, for Ayer, did not need to be verifiable because they are emotions and therefore non-cognitive.

▶Criticisms of Emotivism

—*Why have moral arguments?* One of the criticisms of Emotivism has been the claim that by reducing morals to opinions it rules out any possibility of debate. Consider the situation where Keeley and Oliver are discussing whether lying is wrong. Keeley says 'boo' to lying (she doesn't like it) whereas Oliver says 'hooray' to lying (as long as you can get away with it). According to Emotivism that is it: there can be no further discussion because morals are not facts and there is no correct or incorrect view. However, an emotivist may agree with this analysis but say that there can still be arguments in ethics: there are factual questions (such as 'what is the consequence of lying?') that need to be considered and discussed because the answers to these questions may influence opinion.

—*How can we decide between two people?* Another way to put this problem is to consider many peoples' reaction to the argument between Keeley and Oliver. Even after they have expressed their opinions it still seems possible to ask the question whether we should lie or not. Many people would still want to ask who was correct. This should be a meaningless question according to Emotivism because morals are not facts.

—*Aren't reasons important?* If ethics are based solely on emotions, then presumably the reasons why people have that emotion are not important. This does not seem to fit in with most people's views of ethics where people could have a similar opinion but have it for different reasons. Consider the example of abortion: someone might approve of abortion because it might help a woman out of a very difficult situation; someone else may approve of abortion because they love murder and destruction. Surely these reasons are different in quality and should be taken into account.

—*Couldn't I go out and do what I want?* Emotivism doesn't really provide any solid reason as to why we should be moral. If there is no reason to be moral why can't someone go out and kill anyone she/he wants? It is not 'wrong' if she/he feels that this is right.

—*Problems with Ayer's general philosophy.* There is also another major problem with Ayer's approach in that his entire philosophy has been criticized. It is generally agreed, for example, that his criterion of meaning (that something has to be verifiable in order to be meaningful) is wrong. This may effect Ayer's analysis of ethics as he does rely on this criterion.

▶ **2. Relativism. ('Right depends on where you live.')**

Every culture and every country has different customs and practices.

Some philosophers have argued that morals are simply ways for different cultures to express what they approve or disapprove of. In many ways this theory is similar to Emotivism except that it takes a cultural rather than an individual perspective. This theory that morals are relative (dependent on where you are) is called Relativism or sometimes Cultural Relativism. The immediate consequence of this theory is that there are no absolutes: nothing has to be true in every culture. Morality changes: it depends on where, when and who you are. Cultural Relativism is a non-cognitive theory because, like Emotivism, moral statements are statements of opinion rather than facts.

▶ **Criticisms of Relativism.**

—*Is it consistent?* Relativism suggests that morals are relative to a particular context. However, there does seem to be one idea that is completely unchanging and that is relativism itself! Some philosophers have, therefore, suggested that the theory is logically inconsistent.

—*Others can't be criticized.* The biggest problem with the idea of relativism has been the fact that other countries' morals cannot be described as 'wrong'; they can only be described as 'different'. However, many people would want to describe what other cultures do as wrong. Consider, for example, a country whose culture is based on the eating of babies. According to relativism this practice is not wrong (because 'wrongness' is merely relative to the culture you happen to be in). However, a lot of people would say that it was. In other words this is not how many people want to use moral language. [This is very similar to some of the criticisms of Emotivism. Indeed this sort of problem has really been at the heart of more general criticisms of Subjectivism.]

—*What's society?* Some philosophers have also suggested that it is very unclear what is meant by society. Does any society have any one set of moral codes? What about sub-cultures within society? Do they have their own moral codes or not?

—*What if I disagree?* According to relativism morals are what society approves of. However, this does not allow for any individual disagreeing with any particular society's morals. Relativism provides no mechanism for resolving such disputes.

▶3. An Alternative View. ('Right is what we create it to be.')

A very different approach to morality was developed by the philosopher Nietzsche (1844-1900). In some ways his ideas seem to be similar to sociological approaches. His ideas were also developed by other philosophers in the 20th Century.

Nietzsche attempted to analyse the meaning of the word 'right'. The meaning of 'right' for Nietzsche comes from the 'herds' (the common masses) who are jealous and resentful of the 'aristocrats' (the nobles). Thus there are two types of morality: that of the 'master' and that of the 'slave'. Organized systems of morality, according to Nietzsche, belong to the slaves; what people should be aiming to do is to rise above this slave morality and create better and higher values for themselves. Nietzsche describes this as going beyond Good and Evil. Good, evil, right and wrong are creations of the masses and it is a weakness to follow them. Strength comes from creating for yourself. (This is a theme found throughout Nietzsche's philosophy. It is often expressed as it is our *will to power* that can make us higher people.)

Thus for Nietzsche there is no 'ultimate truth' (and for Nietzsche this is not only the case in ethics it is true for all aspects of philosophy). Indeed his views are often known as 'moral nihilism'. This sort of thinking can be seen in the work of philosophers such as Sartre (1905-1980). These philosophers are usually labelled as Existentialists and their ideas are referred to as Existentialism. The approach taken by Sartre, and others, is that to follow a system of morality is a self-delusion and what we should do is create ourselves and our own moralities in order to be 'authentic'. Indeed everything in itself is meaningless and we have to create our own meaning.

▶Criticisms of this approach.

—*Can you create something 'better'?* This sort of approach seems to suggest that it is 'better' to follow a particular course of action (e.g. following a master morality or being authentic). However, 'better' is itself a value judgement. Thus it could be argued that, to make sense, there must be some sort of moral fact i.e. that fact that it is better to be a master or authentic. However, this is not consistent with the general philosophy.

—*Is there any reason to be moral?* This sort of approach does not seem to give any real reason to be moral. What if it isn't 'better' (either physically or psychologically) for you to follow these ideas? Surely, in that instance it does make sense for you to do it. Another way of putting this is that these theories seem to be psychological: they are about humans and how humans can develop. In a sense this makes them scientific and open to question.

WHAT IS THE DIFFERENCE BETWEEN 'RIGHT' AND 'GOOD'?

There are really two key words that are used when describing morals: right and good. These two words can often be used interchangeably i.e. to ask the question 'what is good?' will often give exactly the same answer to the question 'what is right?'. However, there are some differences in meaning between the two words. Thus far the word 'good' has been deliberately avoided. How is its meaning different from the meaning of the word 'right'?

Perhaps the most immediate difference between right and good is that they seem to refer to slightly different things. Actions and behaviour can be described as right; whereas good seems to refer to human characteristics. Consider Susan who is helping a village in a developing country to build a school. Most people would say that this action was right. However, whilst the action may also be good, the reason that the action is good is that it is the sort of action that a good person would do. Put more simply Susan could be described as being a good person. However, she would not be described as a right person: only her action could be described as right.

Another slight difference between the two words is that good is a comparative word whereas right is not. Something might be good but it could also be better or even best (if it is compared to other things). However, this is not true of the word right: something is either right or not, it cannot be 'righter'.

In a different vein, consider the situation in which an action is described as not wrong. The implication of this is that the action must be right: an action cannot be neither right nor wrong. However, an action can be described as neither good nor bad. In other words if an action is not good, this does not necessarily mean that it is bad.

In the above section, *What does the word 'right' mean?*, the word 'good' could have been substituted. For example, hedonism could be described as a theory that states that what is good is what gives pleasure.

WHAT IS THE NATURE OF MORAL LANGUAGE?

This is one of the questions at the heart of metaethics and really the answer to it is found in the above sections. Indeed another way of looking at the meaning of the word right is to consider the nature of moral language. 'Right' is simply a specific example of moral language and anything that has been said about its meaning could be applied to most moral words.

A number of key ethical terms have already been identified, including good, right, bad, wrong, ought and should. These could be looked at specifically, as in the last two sections, or general comments could be made about them. In making general comments about all ethical words the nature of moral language itself is being examined.

In examining what ethical language is all about the following issues need to be considered:

Does moral language refer to fact or opinion? I.e. is it cognitive or non-cognitive? Another popular way of putting this question is to ask whether moral statements have 'truth value' i.e. whether they can be true or false. A further expression of this question is to ask whether 'ought' (that which should be) implies 'is' (that which happens to be) i.e. whether morals tell us something about the way things are. Indeed this question can also be turned around to ask whether ought can be derived from is. Thus there are many different ways of asking this question.

Does moral language describe or does it instruct us what to do? (Linked to this is the question as to whether moral terms are universalizable. This leads on to the work of Hare.)

Does moral language mean the same in all situations or can it change?

The discussion about these questions can be found in the section on the meaning of the word right. For example, the main argument for cognitivism (the belief that morals are facts) is that what is right and wrong can be discovered. (In other words ought can be derived from is.) In order to do this, however, it is necessary to rely on certain assumptions e.g. that the only thing good in itself is pleasure (Hedonism). If this is assumed, then what is right and wrong can be discovered (and is therefore a fact) because it is possible to discover what is pleasurable. In contrast to this other philosophers, such as Ayer, have argued that it is not possible to discover what is right or wrong since moral statements are not about facts they are merely about opinions.

SHOULD WE ACT MORALLY?

The question as to whether humans should act morally is another major question of metaethics. The nature of moral language and certain ethical theories have already been examined. However, there is still a question that underlies each theory: does it give a reason for being moral? If it doesn't, why should anyone actually bother following the theory?

This is not an easy question to answer. Some philosophers have gone even further and suggested that it does not even make any sense to ask the question. The question is as to why should people be moral. Some philosophers have argued that the word 'should' here can only be meant in a moral sense i.e. it is an 'ought': something people must do. However, this would make the question 'why should people be moral?' a moral question itself. This is circular and therefore some philosophers have suggested that it is not meaningful to ask whether people should be moral. [A really clear example of a 'circular argument' is the argument that the Bible is true because it says so in the Bible.] Such circular arguments do not and cannot prove anything.

However, there are still a number of reasons given by philosophers as to why people should be moral. In addition many of these ideas can also be seen as reasons as to why people are moral. One of these is a concept that lies at the heart of Hedonism and Utilitarianism. It is the belief that being moral is in everyone's own interest. It is argued that it is in everyone's own interest to act morally because everyone will benefit from this. Thus the reason for being moral is that it is in our own interest. This theory is usually known as Egoism. ('Ego' is another word for the self.)

The usual argument for Egoism is that human beings are rational i.e. they think clearly and logically. It is argued that it is irrational to act in such a way that you do not benefit yourself; for example, it does not make sense to deliberately injure yourself for no reason. Thus, to be rational, human beings have to act in such a way that they promote their own interests and put themselves first.

The immediate problem with Egoism as an explanation for why

people should be moral is that self-interest does not seem to be what morality is all about. Consider the situation in which Martin wants to help his friend with her homework. Many people would want to say that this is a morally correct act. However, it does not really seem to be in Martin's interest to do this. An Egoist might respond to this by saying that in the long term it might be in Martin's interest because his friend may stay his friend and may do the same for him one day: it is a bit like a long term self-interested investment.

A development of Egoism that explains why there are moral rules is the idea of Social Contract. This is another very ancient theory, indeed it was around during the time of Plato. One of its most famous exponents, however, was the English philosopher Thomas Hobbes (1588-1679). Hobbes began by describing what he called a 'State of Nature': a place where there was no rules or laws. In such a place life, according to Hobbes, would be difficult as people would be free to kill each or steal from each other or whatever. Indeed Hobbes famously described the state of nature as being 'nasty, brutish and short.' (Thomas Hobbes, *Leviathan*.) It is in our own interest, argues Hobbes, to develop agreements or contracts between each other so that we are protected. ('I won't kill you, if you don't kill me.') This, for Hobbes, is the beginning of government and also the justification why there are rules and laws: there is a social contract which we are all bound to.

In a sense the theory of Social Contract, which has been discussed and developed by a number of philosophers, does not really give a reason why we should be moral. Imagine, for example, the situation in which the 'social contract' goes against your own interests; there may be no reason here for you to be moral. However, there are possibly other reasons why people should be moral. The first may be fear of punishment. If you do something wrong, then you might be punished. In many ways this is just a different way of seeing the idea of self-interest: it is not in your own interest to be punished.

Whilst the fear of punishment may seem a reasonable explanation of why people follow laws it is not obvious how it applies to the whole of morality. For example, I might stick to the speed limit for fear of being caught and fined. However, what 'fear' do I have if I do not help a stranger if I see her/him in difficulty? One suggestion has been that it is conscience which makes us not do things: if we do something wrong, or fail to do something we think that we should do, we might feel guilty about it. This raises an immediate problem, however, in that it is not obvious where conscience comes from. If it is just things that we have learnt from our childhood, this does not give any real reason to follow it. Alternatively some have suggested that conscience is the 'voice of God' and it is God's way of telling humans what to do and what not to do.

The idea of God is in fact given as another reason for being moral. If God exists and judges humans after they die, then there might be a genuine reason to fear doing the wrong thing because there may be some 'ultimate' punishment, such as Hell. This position clearly, however, does rely on the assumption that God exists.

WORKSHEET

1. **For each of the following statements say whether it is a fact or an opinion. Give a brief reason for each of your answers.**

    (i) London is a big city.
    (ii) London is the best city.
    (iii) Buckingham Palace is in London.
    (iv) You should do your homework.
    (v) Manchester City is a good football team.
    (vi) If you do well, you will be rewarded.
    (vii) Human beings are free.
    (viii) The moon orbits the earth.
    (ix) Given a choice between chocolate and crisps, most people would choose crisps.
    (x) It is good to look after your family.

2. **For each of the following pair of words, state how they are similar and how they are different. Try to give an example of what each might say is a right and what each might say is wrong action.**

    Naturalism and Prescriptivism
    Emotivism and Cultural Relativism
    Hedonism and Utilitiariansim
    Intuitionism and Emotivism
    Objectivism and Subjectivism.

3. **Consider the following story:**

    There is a woman who is trying to get to America so that she can be with her future husband. She has no money so she goes to a number of places for help. She firsts goes to the government but they refuse saying that she has not paid enough tax recently. She then tries a friend who also says that she cannot help because the money she has is for her own family. The woman also writes to a rich person who is another person who replies no; this time it is because he can see no benefits for himself. Finally she meets a man in a bar who offers to pay for her flight if she sleeps with him. She is so desperate to see her future husband that she agrees to it. On the flight she decides that the right thing for her to do is own up to her man on arrival in America. However, when she does this her man is so upset he decides to call off the wedding.

(i) Who is the most moral person or group in this story? Give reasons for your answer. (This is in fact a good question to discuss.)

(ii) Look back at all the different ethical theories in this booklet.(E.g. Utilitarianism, Intuitionism, Emotivism.) What do you think that each of them might say about each of the people in the story? I.e. do you think that they would say acted correctly or not? Give reasons for your answer.

---

4. **See if you can explain why it does make sense to ask the question: why should I be rational? How is it similar or different to the question: why should I be moral?**

EXAM QUESTIONS

Exam questions on ethics tend to focus on one particular area, such as ethical language or normative ethics. It sounds obvious but the most important thing to do is to answer the question. One way of attempting to do this is at the end of writing each paragraph ask the question, 'What has this got to do with the title?'. Once you have thought about this write it at the end of the paragraph, so that the examiner is clear how the question has been answered.

It is also very important to plan your essay. This will help give you the necessary structure in order to answer the question. Consider the following examples:

Can what 'ought to be' be derived from 'what is'?

INTRODUCTION
    What the question means: essentially are morals facts (i.e. what we should do can be found out) or are they opinions?

OUGHT CAN BE DERIVED FROM IS
    Arguments: we can discover what is right and wrong i.e. what we ought to do.
    How? Attempts to do this include:
    Naturalism (Hedonism) etc.
    Intuitionism etc.

PROBLEMS WITH THIS IDEA
    There are specific problems with these theories e.g. naturalistic fallacy.

OUGHT CANNOT BE DERIVED FROM IS
    Arguments: attempts to derive is from ought do not work; we cannot know.
    Why not? Morality is about opinions—a very different order of language.
    Examples of this idea include: Relativism and Emotivism

PROBLEMS WITH THIS IDEA
Problems with Relativism and Emotivism e.g. why have moral debate?

CONCLUSION
What is the most convincing position?

Give a critical account of Naturalism.

INTRODUCTION
What is naturalism?
Naturalistic theories e.g. hedonism and Utilitarianism

STRENGTHS OF NATURALISM
Gives an explanation of where morality comes from
Ensures that morality can be discovered i.e. is a fact.
Examples of this include pleasure.
Makes morality more of a science.

WEAKNESSES OF NATURALISM
Problems with the theory e.g. facts cannot be discovered.
Naturalistic fallacy.
What is natural?

CONCLUSION
Is Naturalism a realistic theory?

FURTHER READING

Many general introductions to philosophy, some of which are listed here, contain a chapter or chapters on ethical theory and are worth having a look at. Another useful source can be dictionaries of philosophy, which often have some very good articles about different ethical theories. Do be careful, however, when looking at books on ethics as many do tend to focus on practical ethics (moral problems) rather than ethical theory. It can also be worthwhile reading the original works of many of the philosophers mentioned in this booklet: many are very readable.

Philosophy: the basics.
By Nigel Warburton (Routledge 1992)
Readability: *** Content: ###
Provides a good outline of the main ideas and theories found in ethics.

Mastering Philosophy.
By Anthony Harrison-Barbet (MacMillan 1990)
Readability: * Content: ###
Contains a very detailed discussion of particular philosopher's ethical theories. These discussions are very usefully based on the original texts of those philosophers.

Philosophy.
Mel Thompson (Teach Yourself Books 1995)
Readability: *** Content: #
Provides some good examples of different ethical theories as well as a good summary of some of the main ethical ideas.

Ethics.
By Peter K. McInerney and George W. Rainbolt
(Harper Collins 1994)
Readability: **** Content: ###
A very readable account which covers most of the topics in ethics very well.

The Puzzle of Ethics.
By Peter Vardy and Paul Grosch (Fount 1994)
Readability: *** Content: ###
A good introduction with some interesting perspectives.

Moral Maze.
By David Cook (SPCK 1983)
Readability: *** Content: ##
Whist this book is mostly about Christian ethics, the early general sections are very good and provide a good introduction to ethical theory.

An Introduction to Ethics.
By J.D. Mabbot (Hutchinson and Co. 1966)
Readability: * Content: ####
A classic introduction which contains a good detailed discussion of most ethical theories.

KEY   Readability   * manageable;   ** good;
              *** very good;   **** excellent.

          Content   # adequate;   ## good;
              ### very good;   #### excellent.

GLOSSARY

Absolute—always, unquestionably true.

Cognitive—something that can be perceived i.e. can be true or false.

Consequentialism—another word for teleological.

Deontological—literally 'concerned with duty'; based on means.

Descriptive—something that indicates what's there.

Egoism—theory that humans are self-interested i.e. work for their own ends.

Emotivism—theory that morals are based on emotions.

Ends—the outcomes.

Hedonism—theory that states that what is right is happiness.

Intuitionism—theory that states that morals are based on our intuitions.

Means—how something is achieved.

Naturalism—theory that states that morals are based on some aspect of nature.

Non-cognitive—something that cannot be perceived i.e. is neither true nor false.

Objective—true, factual.

Prescriptive—something that gives an instruction.

Relative—dependent upon something else.

Subjective—internal, personal, based on opinion.

Teleological—literally 'concerned with ends'.

Utilitarianism—theory that states that what is right is the greatest happiness of the greatest number.

NOTES